the archive is all in present tense

Cover Art: Dorothy Hoover.
Cover Photograph: Gavin Benjamin
Cover & Book Design: Zoe Norvell

Published 2022 by Barrow Street, Inc.
(501) (c) 3) corporation. All contributions are tax deductible.
Distributed by:
Barrow Street Books
P.O. Box 1558
Kingston, RI 02881

Barrow Street Books are also distributed by Small Press Distribution,
SPD, 1341 Seventh Street Berkeley, CA 94710-1409, spd@spdbooks.
org; (510) 524-1668, (800) 869-7553 (Toll-free within the US); amazon.
com; Ingram Periodicals Inc., 1240 Heil Quaker Blvd, PO Box 7000,
La Vergne, TN 37086-700 (615) 213-3574; and Armadillo & Co., 7310
S. La Cienega Blvd, Inglewood, CA 90302, (310) 693-6061.

Special thanks to the University of Rhode Island English Department
and especially the PhD Program in English, 60 Upper College Road,
Swan 114, Kingston, RI 02881, (401) 874-5931, which provides
valuable in-kind support, including graduate and undergraduate interns.

First Edition

Library of Congress Control Number: 2022940256

ISBN: 978-1-7366075-5-8

the archive is all in present tense

elizabeth hoover

BARROW STREET PRESS

NEW YORK CITY

Contents

Part III: See Also

Acknowledgments

sometimes the archive is a spring snow

Sometimes the archive is as opaque as an oracle.
Sometimes it plays as easy as a music box.

Sometimes it's a dentist chair and long novocaine needle.
Sometimes it freezes over, and I watch librarians labor under ice.

Sometimes the archive is a museum of Fabergé eggs and
    ingenious watches.

Sometimes it doesn't exist, and the Archivist and I sit in the
    wheat dreaming up history.

Sometimes it's the prescience of the riot.
Sometimes a wall of windows overlooking a Permian swamp.

Today the archive is an aquarium. Bass
glide in and out of the stacks, catfish carry paper

in their whiskers, eels swarm at the catalog's open
drawers. A librarian in a bathysphere leads a trout to my table.

The trout looks like an ancient mechanism dragged
from the sludge with a sorrowful mouth and bristled tongue,

extravagantly speckled and pink on its underside. When I slide
my page slip free of her gills, I see the velvet red

of her breathing apparatus. Bubbles spill, jaw
grinds open, and her mouth gapes as if she is answering

every question I came here with or drowning
on a dock after a girl yanked her from the pond wanting

to see what would happen if she counted
to a hundred before tossing her back.

Part I: Material Culture

Memories can cohere around objects in unpredictable ways, and the task of an archivist of emotion is thus an unusual one.
—*Ann Cvetkovich*

Subjects   material culture--archival resources
material culture--classification
material culture--collection and preservation
material culture--deterioration
ephemera--themes, motives
psychological disorders--perseveration,
   obsession
psychological disorders--haptic
paraphilia--paper objects

the archive is all in present tense

Librarians turn slender shadows in the afternoon light
gathering materials along the ledge. Three men exit
a Jeep on a hill side, doors slam in unison. Two orphans
walk into a dance for soldiers. Wind winters down
from the north. Concertina wire unspools
like fat loops of cursive, *I've always wanted*
a boyfriend like you language making it impossible
for her to love me back, though no one could love
me now, preoccupied as I am by war, paging
arrest records, letters, diaries, clippings
in their acid-free envelops. I sort through tea lights,
radio crackles, paper fortune tellers predicting the man
who will marry you, what house he will buy
for you, paper turning to snow in her hands
folding, unfolding.

                     After the librarians bring
the snow I check if they are watching, then touch the jars,
feel the cold of silence, of waiting. The men pass
concertina wire hand-to-hand as trucks convey
people up the mountain. One orphan creases
his hat, the other smooths her pleats, practices
American slang, a letter turns over to an empty
verso, a blank my want tumbles into. The archive is full
of blanks. So many archivists come before dawn
to catalog them and are still behind.

Librarians bring everything I write on a call slip
without judgement or warning. I write *en masse.*
I write *war bride*, I write *amnesty*, I write *savagery*
is the natural condition of the human race, I write
I can't keep my men from the refugee women.

I page dirt from the camp floor, blankets
and hunger, sickness and sorrow. I could page
his service records or the stories he told
about how his commanders liked him *so much, they kept
me from all that.* I could page the women's voices
in their velvet bags bound with string. The archive is full
of string, full of wire and casings and food stamp books
and adoption records and wills and transfer requests.
The archive is full of tanks and spears and muskets
and porcelain and dollars and steamboats and axes
and folly and fall. Cataloged, so I can page it all.

BL 468
1986   assortment of paper fortune tellers.
               --a few hints to social relations among teen
               girls.--Pittsburgh, Pa.--1986-1997 (approx.).

               16 v : acid free envelope
               title devised by cataloger

materials--biodegration
see also: paper deterioration
narrower term--rag paper--deterioration
unrelated term: parietal art

dactyloscopy
see also: friction ridge skin impres.
see also: merocrine glands

simple machines
narrower term: levers
narrower term: pulleys
see also: simple machines at work

declared death in abstentia
see also: absence and presumption of death
see also: civil death
see also: missing persons

the archive is full of deferrals

Today I request death sentences. The librarian accepts
my stack of page slips, leads me to a table, asks me to don
an apron and mask before wheeling in carts of lead boxes.
Each sentence is about the size of an ear of corn, twice
as heavy and smooth, graphite-colored. They make me
draw my shoulders back, grow a belly, walk like a general
surveying lines of refugees, taste the iron of my promise. I check

them against front pages: masked blur of a woman braced
in a chair, hooded face of a boy unable to bow
to the altar of bread and chewing gum, engraving
of men hanging in a town square. A death sentence
sparkles dust onto the clippings. Somewhere,
in off-site storage, pardons and commutations, possibilities
of parole are stacked like drawers in a mausoleum.

Outside light slides under field. Librarians wait.
I page a box dated the day after a kid from Detroit
joked with a chaplain in Northern France. Librarians
rush to the stacks. The box is weightless, empty
except for a glow that smells cool and wet
like the Marathon station's cement where my corsage
drops its white flag. We convince some trucker
to buy us beer and drink in the lot until our mouths
taste like rotten wheat. Then a grey Chevy pulls in—
my sister and her friends, all older, too old
for the dance. They look like Spring in sundresses
and halters. We share our beer and my sister's friend
has silver earrings that sparkle to her bare shoulders.
She leads me from the station's light. Her hand
is cool and damp and her breath bitter and warm.
I breathe it in as long as I can before I know
it's time—I have to kiss her.

the archive husbands time

Today the archive is the empty chambers of the dead
nautilus boiled clean. Pages whisper like lovers
in a language I can't identify. Crows tell all
they witness. I transcribe their cackles, telegram
orthologists, study cuneiform fractures
in a hunger-weakened bone cataloged under
inscriptions--osteology--bride, double
check *Introduction to Sumerian Grammar*
but my translation keeps reading *a boyfriend
like you, really no one was ever nice to me
but I can't tell any.* Swaying by the reshelving station,
librarians fold used call slips into fortune
tellers, pointing at their chosen flaps. I gather

my notes, collect my bag from the hallway locker.
In the parking lot an archivist makes a show of looking
for their keys. I try a friendly *hello* but it's laced
with defeat. "Consider time," they say like a typewriter.
"Out here one thing happens after another, causal
or not—anywhere along that spectrum." Their cheeks sparkle
under circular glasses, as if they swiped graphite
on for blush. "In the archive, time submits
to the catalog. Out here," they motion like bailing
up wire. "Time is master." I step closer to examine
their bowtie. Whirring Kodachrome?
Reel-to-reel tape? They lean back, light
in their spectators. "Good luck," they type
into the wind and duck into their car, leaving me
in a blank landscape—timeless as an FSA photograph.

the archive falls as silent as snow

The librarians reshelve the passing
season, desks mounded with clumsy flowers, air
peppered with pollen, huffy bees shooed
into apiaries. I am buried under a morning's
worth of paging: a John Wayne poster taped
to a Jeep's glove box, airmail love letters between
orphans, her third time asking if there will ever
be a plane ticket, divorce papers, white hoods
of clergy, even my sister's paper on symbolism
in Fitzgerald. *Gatsby wore white for his reunion*
with Daisy to display his purety, she writes for a D.

I stopped writing her papers after she caught me
in a thrift-store tux having struggled out of tulle
in our grandfather's cream Buick. *I won't tell anyone*
else, she begged, *please just help me.* My silence fell
like an October snow, so sudden the pioneer woman knew
her husband would be trapped at the ranch, wood soaked
through. She slaughtered the ox herself, dragged it
inside, nestled her children between steaming lungs
where their father found them, chipped them free. How
strange to be reborn from an ox, your father a midwife,
your mother a statue, your afterbirth precious stone.

A mound of goldenrod topples and librarians rush
to prop it up. They drop to their knees,
shimmy leaves into envelopes, brush blossoms
onto sheets of paper. I sneak into the stacks, run
my hands along metal shelves, hoping to find a trail
of algae, a bit of pond water. At the corridor's end, light
from a small room where the Archivist bends over
a desk, stringing bones on wire, fashioning

marionettes. Without turning, they draw
a sheet over their work and a ribbon spools
from their mouth. I SEE YOU'VE COME
LOOKING FOR THE TAXIDERMY COLLECTION.

E181

.86   jar containing 236 cm3 snow
                includes handwritten note--manche,
                france--unhoused

frostbite cold--adverse effects
see also: cold--physiological effects
see also: cold adaptation

restraint of prisoners--handbooks, manual, etc.
restraint of prisoners--equipment and supplies
handcrafts--collectibles

recovered memory
see also: delayed memory
see also: recovered memories
see also: sacred space--conservation and restoration

optics and photonics--problems
narrower term: black body radiation
narrower term: diffraction
narrower term: dispersion

narrower term: light deflectors
narrower term: invisibility

only rugged mountaineers live in the archive

I marvel at the taxidermist's precision, flesh
pinned open like a bloom, bristles of the cub's
tongue dewy with blood. The Archivist beckons
and I follow, wondering at my quiet ally, how
they stay apart from the others, their affinity
for bones, their familiarity as if they found me
long ago cataloged under adolescent daydreams,
childhood hurts. I stumble against coyotes dangling
a work shirt from ruddy jaws and cry out.

The Archivist covers my mouth. "Hush,"
they say, index finger perched on the notch
of my upper lip, cool as ballpeen hammer,
and gesture into the vaulted dark where a mountain
lion perches on a column, rabbit clasped between paws.
Their fingers knit into mine, keeping me tight
to their side as we walk by *denizens of the forest,*
sovereigns of the desert, sages of the artic,
inhabits of the many-mooded ocean.

Crates of caribou antlers, stacks of tortoise shell,
a whale's jawbone we pass beneath
like a bower, hibernacula sliced
from the ground, sleeping snouts mist
glass. Two mournful musk oxen guard
a door the Archivist opens with keys
muffled in a leather case. Inside we skate

across a diorama's wavered glass to a mannequin
draped in deer skin, a giant trout on a spear lifted
from the water. We kneel at the mannequin's feet
and the Archivist taps the fish, its mouth spills

red dust. I hold my breath. There, the Archivist's
palm on the back of my neck, I know
it's time—I have to ask them.

In the Archive of Possible Utterances

I know it's time—I have to ask them
about my grandfather laughing, *my commanders*
liked me so much they kept me from all that, women

huddled on the mountain, concertina wire
respooled after the camp was cleared. Instead
I offer the verso of a note I never

answered from a girl I met at a gas station
who wanted someone to be nice to her and only
knew the word *boyfriend* to ask for it. I offer

the gravel driveway her brother dragged her down.
My silence is the screwdriver I use to open
the front of the Archivist's throat revealing

a mouthpiece from a portable radio transmitter.
When I press my mouth against it, I kiss my own
ghosts and the echoes of all we never became.

TJ
1015
.H66   Unknown

possible utterance--compact cassette tape--ca. 1996-1963-present--1/8" magnetic tape (polyester-based tape with ferromagnetic particles embedded in binder layer) attached to take-up reels enclosed in plastic case--Dolby noise reduction, stereo, quarter track con-figuration--1 7/8" (1.875) isp

compressed air
see also: pressure vessels
vacuum--history

conveying machinery
narrower term: bulk solids handling
narrower term: pneumatic-tube transportation

see also: orienting mechanism
see also: mental derangements
see also: study of sexes in society
see also: sexual practices viewed as medical disorder

disorientation

channels of distribution
diversion structures
umbras and penumbras

fate and fatalism
narrower term: fortune

narrower term: necessity

cloud physics
touch
narrower term: haptic sense

anoxemia
narrower term: after-sensation
narrower term: perceptual disorder

TJ
1015
.H66

We are only pneumatic tubes shuttling information.

Only the question information leaves, the shadow of something
passing. Look up—empty sky.

The question left by the buttermilk scar along a girl's knee where
nurses swabbed the wound free of gravel and sewed up her
imagined future.

We are only the question: when the fog lifts will there be snow
on the mountain?

The question of the palm turned and not its meaning: plea,
prayer, offering, or reaching to feel if snow is falling.

Only the palm turned waiting for someone to reach across the
distance from bed to chair.

Only the creak of the chair and the tick tick of moons dropping
from bag to tube.

We are only the crunching of gravel as a car turns into the drive,
headlights sweeping over two girls tangled in shadows.

We are only the waiting for the car door to open.

Waiting like the rabbit waits in the light the motion detector
clicked on.

We are only the ruffle of fur above her heart as she waits for the
dark so she can scatter.

We are only the grip turning a girl's hand white as she yanks
away in the light.

Only the burn of nerves as the blood returns, the itch of it, hot
as guilt.

the archive sings all winter

cases of sparrows with cotton eyes;
redwings pinned mid-flight; flesh
from the teeth of buzzards; tawny blur
of goldfinch in cornstalks; gibberish
of starlings decoded by Dutch scientists;
tricks of mockingbirds on amateur naturalists;
blue jays; whippoorwill; wariness of the fulvous;
pulsing coo of loon; piracy of frigate; owls
in night boxes; the caw of killdeer; muteness
of swans; waders and plovers; vagrants and migrants;
graceful and graceless; genus and species; flightless
and frantic; cages for the living and boxes for the dead.

sometimes the archive sculpts vermin from marble

A librarian capsizes on my table, drunk
on the dust of wine, accordion wheezing
like a racoon scissored in a trap, papers
scatter, music sours as they fall
out of time.

"What are we celebrating?"
I ask another librarian at the front desk, picnic
basket poised on their knees. They remind
me to note my seat number on the page slip
though—as always—I am the only one here.

When they bring me my box, I notice
their palms are stained grey, remember the executions
I paged earlier. People came from all over
to watch, each hanging a festival, every
electrocution a party.

The Boys' Book of Adventure
embossed on the book's green leather cover, I finger
the gold edges of its pages, then open to engravings
of two grubby tomboys clamoring over rocks, my sister
cups a crawdaddy, knee skinned raw.

On the next page, we are playing war, I wear
my grandfather's helmet, brandish a stick
for a gun. I can't bring myself to turn
the page, imagining the dresses and distance
that came with puberty. In the parking lot,

I look for the Archivist,
wanting to commiserate about the silliness

of history. It's empty except for a possum
lumbering across the asphalt, dragging
its naked tail. "Hey," I call. "What does it all
add up to?" It freezes and flips over, fleshy feet
stretched to the sky, toothy mouth agape. I toe
around the stiff form and get into my car, crank

the heat, stretch my palms to the vents. My hands
speckled with gilt from the book. With each opening
it must slough off some of its luster.

unprocessed
PR 13 CN
.MC
1968   The Green Berets--movie poster showing battle scene and
         headshots of John Wayne and Jim Hutton—So you don't
         believe in glory. And heroes are out of style. And they don't
         blow bugles anymore. So take another look--at the special
         forces in special kind of hell--creator Frank McCarthy--
         includes handwritten note on verso and $250 USD--84 x 61 cm

Photo print drawing
Vietnam War, 1955-1975

Motion picture posters--American--1960-1970
Prints, color--1960-1970

parents, parenthood
        --including parent and child, husbands, fathers, wives, mothers
see also: connubial relations, transitory
narrower term: breach of promise
narrower term: desertion

See also: gods--absent

soil dynamics
see also: soil fertility
see also: soil fumigation
see also: soil freezing
see also: detritus
see also: erosion

materials
narrower term: bulk solids
narrower term: coatings
narrower term: friction materials
narrower term: granular materiality

narrower term: heat resistant materials
narrower term: materials at low temperature
narrower term: rubble
narrower term: surplus

speculative term--keep walking
Narrower term: cat ripping up rabbits
Narrower term: eel curved by current
Narrower term: kid with a fort on an empty beach
Narrower term: woman without wishes for husband's return

in the archive you need a name

The clerk sawed off syllables, tossed
consonants, stitched in vowels, made
a chimera that licked its bloody chops
on every page of my grandfather's

military records. He changed it after
the war, named himself after the Greek man
the nuns said invented history. Nothing
cataloged under that but silence. His silences

come in foam-lined boxes too heavy
to lift. They are ruckled and veined, stippled
and scaled. Some have spines and beveled edges.
Some scarred where the tool slipped. I take off

my gloves, press my bare hands to the slabs,
and a librarian rushes over tsking like a kettle.
In my car, I press my palms against my face, breathe
in oil, wrenches, gaskets, and valves. Breathe in

coffee tins punched with holes for re-oiling
nuts and screws. Breathe in arithmetic scrawled
on carboard. My grandfather's silences aren't
silent. They are shuffles and coughs, scrape of metal,

rattle of cans. They are tapping his fingers
as he studies charts of torque values
and tolerances. His silences are *let's see here*
and *leave that girl alone* and my silences

are their counterweight, their ballast, block
and tackle. If I paged my own name, the librarians
would bring boxes of feathers, inscribed
on their spines: *ask while he is still alive.*

Part II: Narrower Terms

While seriously engaged in establishing an archive of queerness, [the queer act] simultaneously disrupts the very notion of official subsidized and substantiated institutions.
—José Esteban Muñoz

Subjects   teenage girls--care
teenage girls--mental health
teenage girls--sexual behavior--public opinion
teenage girls--social life and customs
teenage girls--wounds and injuries
gay teenagers--care--social aspects
hate crimes--moral and ethical aspects
homosexuality--Christianity--United States--
     religious aspects
androgyny (psychology) in art

the archive maestros history

"You can't go in like that," the Archivist's teletype hooks
me in the parking lot. They hand me a suit bag, turn
as I unzip—net of tulle, the dress strains against

my shoulders. I smell the licorice my grandfather
chewed to quit tobacco, shutter shushing as I stepped
into the cream Buick. The Archivist, in a tux and tails

pinstriped with sprocket holes, slides a putrid corsage
on my wrist, gathers my elbow. The lobby is packed
with gowns and jackets swollen by the absence

of their owners. Hatpins, stays, and cravats stream
past as I tug at my clinging hem and find
a satin stripe, a pocket my hand easily slips into.

The Archivist plucks cufflinks from the air, fastens
my sleeves and straightens my bowtie. They vanish
with a curtsey into the tremble of velvet draping

the catalog. A pillbox hat hands me a program
that reads *nice to me but I can't tell any of my friends*
about you, how it feels to the paper disintegrates
as instruments lift at the urging of an unseen baton.

ACT I

Vermiculated like a lung, the curtain crumples revealing two swans on a mirror hung three feet from the floor. The catalog hulks in the wings and the trumpet's valves clack in time with the oboe's quivering keys. In the mirror's green shadow, a pile of blood and clothes shudders. Unseen strings lift a woman by her shoulders. She climbs through the mirror shaking river grass from her hair, cradles an eel against her, then releases it into the dark. Another woman stands at the mirror's edge, jimmies a knife from her chest, folds the red billowing from her throat. Twins clasp hands, unwind rope from the other's neck. A young teacher mends her dress, plucking bullets from her ribs while her sister shakes the rounds from her own skull. One-by-one they walk into the stacks. Librarians in black carry the mirror away. The instruments quicken, pistons groaning into airless tubes, and a spotlight clicks on above a Jeep. Three men lean on the hood, arms slung around each other's shoulders. One re-spools film into a Minolta, foot propped on a bail of concertina wire. They face the audience, arms open, bow: center, left, right, center. The instruments lower as the men leave the reading room empty except for its carpet of teeth and a stained work shirt dangling like a question from a girl's mouth.

Intermission

We rise and uncreak the creases.
We rise, applause dislodging dust from doveskin.
We rise and go—silk and tulle, whalebone and waistcoat, pleat
  and pearl.
We rise in chemises and shifts, stockings and redingotes, chintz
  and taffeta and go.

We gather in clutches of sleeves and slacks, cabals of
  houndstooth and hoopskirts, bundles of buckles
  and stomachers.
We spill speeches, lines, mummified wine from goblets and
  glasses, mugs and steins. It stains the lobby floor like
  a bruise roping the wrist.
We are the bones that held the skin that lifted the bodices, that
  blushed beneath fichu, that cooed black Alençon lace, that
  fingered the piping, that pressed its corset against another's
  corsage.

We are the memory of those bones—linen pinched at the knee,
  trumpet sleeves gaping at the elbow, the empty cast trailing
  tendrils of cotton.
We are the recollection of ligament, the ball of muscle at the
  base of the tongue.
We are the Latin of its name.

We are a tide bundled against the shore, bundled against the
  door, straining to get out into the air, into what will make
  us decay—the only way we know to join the living.
We brush against leaving, cradle what remains.

We are hermetic and hermeneutic—dry as a cat's breath, and
    we miss the oil of our owners, their skin and its secretions.
We miss the little girl's spit as she chews on our ribbons in
    church, blood speckling a gym uniform, sweat from the
    orphan's palms as she smooths and smooths her skirt on
    her first plane ride, slender wrists crossed in her lap all the
    way to America.

We powder at the touch, rot on contact, yellow in light.
We want our seams to tear with a fumble, a child to grow out
    of us, a gait to make a side split, frugality to transform us
    into quilt or rag.
We talk with our collars, confound with our stitching, tattle
    with our smell.
We are echoes of flesh and partners of presence.
We are attendants, waiting on you, wanting to be worn again.

ACT II

The scene is a working-class living room in Pittsburgh. Mid-1950s. Lit by a black-and-white television stage left.

[from television]

HOWDY DOODY:
> But Mr. Bluster I have so little left!

MR. BLUSTER:
> Well, you can think about what you want to give me but I mean to collect.

HOWDY DOODY:
> Oh Clarabelle do you have any ideas for what I can give to Mr. Bluster?

[on television: close up of a ledger]

Clarabelle honks horn twice.

Lights up

A puppet theater, hand painted and made of cardboard descends to the stage.

THE ARCHIVIST, *in all black, enters, carrying two marionettes made of bone and gold wire. They take their place behind the puppet theater. The curtains on the puppet theater pull back to reveal a miniature kitchen set and* THE SCOPEDOODLE. THE ARCHIVIST *adjusts the knobs and a film strip comes into focus. The words* "Operation Diaper Run" *flash over the screen, then the image of a couple, shot from below, embracing on a beach. Fade to test pattern.*

THE ARCHIVIST *dangles one marionette onto the stage. The marionette wears a blue-and-white gingham dress, white cap lined in lace, and a white apron. She is swaying back and forth and humming until the second marionette descends suddenly. The second marionette has a red, crescent-shaped hat and carries a Louisville Slugger. The female marionette tries to flee stage right, but the male marionette gains on her and they collide.*

THE ARCHIVIST *drops the female puppet so she clatters to the floor.*

Lights out

[from television]

BUFFALO BOB SMITH:
> Oh geez Clarabelle, I can hear them but I can't see them. Let's try something. Now you come here and tell me what you see.
>
> Hey, kids, what time is it?
>
> Clarabelle, can you see any kids in the Peanut Gallery?

CLARABELLE *honks twice then slowly creeps out of the television and crawls to the puppet theater, where he lifts the curtains, revealing the shattered bones of the marionette.*

CLARABELLE *sweeps the fragments into a shoe box labeled* "Property of Mr. Bluster," *then lets the puppet theater's curtains fall.*

[from television]

BUFFALLO BOB SMITH:
  It's all my fault there aren't any boys and girls!

CLARABELLE *repeatedly honks as the main stage curtains fall.*

Part III: See Also

*The body archive is an attunement, a hopeful gathering, an act
of love against the foreclosures of reason.*
—Julietta Singh

Subjects   domestic relations
marriage
desertion and non-support
abandonment--legal status, laws, etc.
poverty--women
low-income mothers
destitution
domestic relations--criminal provisions
marital relations--law and legislation
osteology
spiral fracture
lunate, cleft, ulna,
osteoclasts--gap healing
healing--language of

The Archive's Archive

is mostly gum the librarians scrape from under the reading
    room tables
and hope trapped in tubes with glass stoppers: a chance discovery,
a suspicion confirmed, a hero nestled in the genealogy
like a blackberry in brambles; candy wrappers swept
from the corner of lockers; thousands of cigarette butts
plucked from the sidewalk by white-gloved hands careful
not to smudge the occasional lipstick stains; pencils sharpened into
nubs or perforated by incisors; the odd nap; the crush
that keeps pulling focus from the material; drawers of blushes
and surprised smiles; deadlines curled and dried in glass-topped
boxes alongside stacks of notes the Archivist uncrumpled,
    smoothed
again and again with their dry palm: *check dates on pgs 15, 24, 17;*
why no mention of S after 1876?; letter dated Sept 4, 1974 smells
strongly of pipe? cigar? check if RH smoked cause of death; diss topic:
female friendship as social control; diss topic: refiguring
violence as language? or resignifying? post-hrc report; the coats;
the intentions; the projects stalled and abandoned; the imprint
of the bodies who come just to sit in the hush and imagine
history unspooling around them, circling to entrap or
    embrace.

the archive romances the records

alleges permanent disability
                          Documents swarm
like fish at feeding
            The shape he is now he is totally
disabled for performance of any manual labor
                                    blurring
as my eyelids grow heavy in the reading room's warmth.

A sliver of sunlight flashes through my fluttering lids
like light at the flap of a tent. I lean against
the center pole, gnawing at a plug of tobacco.

                          keep my men from
the refugee women

                In the shadows beneath
the general's desk, my grandfather crouches, bent
and shackled, unspooling the paper from the telegram
machine, fingers stained black, more ink at the ready.

                                    spread
of disease and the impossibility of getting supplies
up the mountain

                My grandfather shivers
as the telegram clatters, shivers so hard the ink
tumbles from his hands. The Archivist in a green beret
and camo reaches for me, knitting their fingers—thin
as a contrail—into mine as we slide along the ink's greasy spill
into a surprising spring snow. Jerked

awake by cawing, I grasp the edge of the reading room table
to reorient myself, shake the dream free.

not due to

vicious habits

        Crows stalk along the roofbeams,
I sit under the dome of their screeching, clumsy and childish,
as if I was the one who tipped over their cages.

        body poorly nourished,
skin pale, both veins varicose to the knee.

        Librarians
materialize, white gloves fluttering above me. Looking up,
I see an asterisk of light scatter prismatic rainbows above
the reshelving station. The Archivist, all glint and wink,
is tilting a lens.
        I know this from having served
with him and having seen him frequently since the war
was over.
        When I look up again, the Archivist is gone.

I breeze past a frantic librarian, give the pencil sharpener
a few whirls, then slide into the stacks, find the Archivist
hidden under a white parasol in tiered frills.

        "Meet Me in St. Louis?"

I ask, trying to look coquettish.

        "No, the unaccessioned objects room."

Are we doing the same joke? I follow their ruffled skirts,
swear the edges of their petticoats are dipped in gold.

Found in Collection

we are a thing made
into another thing

matchbox   lantern
        doorbell

mouth gapping around the button

                hand
of a whip leg
                of a divan

made into the tool that makes
us awl chisel gouge makes us
compass oar ship bedpost part-
swan part-cow part-cat part-snake
part-truck part-bottle part-car

made to be made
        Victory
        Empire
        Change
        Thorn and Scepter
        Crown

when you pull our tongue we reveal
time   minutes in one eye , hours
in the other   seconds ring from our throat

yank us by the hair and pour us
into goblets made from us   rattle us
before opening   throw us out   trade us
hollow soundless   instrument
for another's mouth

toy puppet doll   arm
        partially broken
                                    face
        partially missing
                                    made
        to be missing   bound
        to end up in some drawer
        somewhere decades later

bound to a tree bound between two trees bound
to a bench bound to a bed bound to a fence bound
to a stable door bound in a trailer bound in a trunk
bound in a boat bound in a basement bound to end
up alone and childless bound to end up in jail bound
to end up dead bound to show up on your doorstep
asking for money show up covered in tattoos show up
now prettier show up wet and willing our first time

we don't have minds souls wishes
we don't have futures plans drives
we don't have scars wounds marks
we don't have blood
we don't have tears
we don't have taste
or tongue   we don't dream

we weren't blessed or cared for kept
        in proper storage humidity controlled
we weren't polished oiled protected
        from sunlight moisture thieves neighbors camp counselors
we were never found or rescued unless
        we were found and rescued written
        into a scholar's list of discoveries
we were never exiled and allowed to return
        welcomed home after injustice revealed

we were never clever when faced
        with an impossible choice
we never kept a cool head in an emergency or
        came up with an ingenious solution to an intractable
        problem

we are the prize given
        to the prodigal prodigy genius hero sleuth

we are a golden statue set of scales candelabra

the chalkboard on which the solution is written
beaker bubbling on a burner
the window someone else stares out of

we are parenthesis brackets close quotes

spaces around an utterance around silence   sputter
as the wick burns down shush of wave sound of ribbon
sliding through a grommet a thing made to be

unmade each remaking leaves   imprint
                                       trace

find us under the hooves of statues of generals
leading an army to glory find us in the extra piece
that mars the puzzle—so docile yet

our excess is relentless   so abject
we become royal   so useless   we destroy logics
and in the space between
                        void and crisis   we are alive with
the resolute thingness of us

HV 4010

.H157   Royal Doulton, mfr.; Harradine, Leslie, desigr.
            The Hinged Parasol, ca. 1933

        Porcelain figure; 6.5 in. x 4x 5in--Early 20th-century
Royal Doulton English Porcelain Figure, "The Hinged Parasol" issued
from 1933-1949. Figure attired in red-and white-dress with matching
parasol. Underside backstamp, numeral 6 and painter's monograph H
for Emma C. Harrison, recorded as working at Doulton in 1933.

        Condition note: in poor condition, face cracked on
diagonal, left foot missing, parasol handle missing, both hands
broken. Glue remnants present.

visual materials
Royal Doulton--figurines--1933-1949

dolls--repairing
see also: doll hospital

social pathology, social criminal welfare
    --protection, assistance and relief, special classes--immigrants
see also: the family--marriage--women--sexual life
see also: military spouses
narrower term: sadism, fetishism etc.

mendacity, vagabonds, tramps
see also: homelessness--psychological aspects
narrower term: homeless mothers

meteorology
atmospheric attenuation
narrower term: noctilucent clouds
narrower term: orographic clouds

phobic disorders--kenophobia

# of what is not written, the archive only dreams

When the archive dreams of Pittsburgh, smoke pours
from the stacks, and librarians don goggles, wrap the books
in tarp. When the archive dreams of Pittsburgh, I perch

on an overhead crane and watch as a silhouette
emerges from a row of hook blocks, shimming
with a pole to flip open the furnace. Molten

spreads along paper under the red light
of a junkie's darkroom. I stumble into the parking lot,
where the Archivist kneels, easing gas masks off

goldfinches. They lean back on their heels, unhook
their collar—already blackened— lift a fresh one
from a nearby briefcase. We are high up

in an office at Gulf Oil unwrapping a roast beef sandwich.
Meanwhile the archive dreams of a woman taking off
her apron, sitting in the quiet, her coffee speckled

with the three drops of cream she allows herself. I want
to sit next to her but even the Archivist's magic only
takes us to the lip of the unrecorded. Once I fell

in love with a woman who'd been a thief. She kept
her juvenile release papers in a box with dried out
Wet n' Wild makeup to remind us how little we have

to take from them. She touched me like a lockpick,
like she was listening for tumblers to click into place.
She touched me as if I wasn't already a gate hanging

from broken hinges. In the parking lot, I finger ruffles
edged in gold on the porcelain doll the Archivist slipped
into my pocket before the librarians joined us.

I remember finding one just like it—or is this the same one?—
amidst scarves and perfume bottles in my grandfather's attic,
an elegant dream of summer blushing under parasols

along an American river, a reminder a woman lived
in this house, made it possible for us to forget her.

in the archive you need a name

"Do you have a name?" the librarian asks, hands
folded atop of a stack of finding aids. "I do, married
name." The librarian takes my slip returns with

a box of tea bags saved for re-use, an apron, pattern
envelope with a woman in a red-and-white dress,
matching parasol. They bring medical records:

a trip, a fall, accidental touch of the iron, a miscarriage.
And before she was married? I don't know that name
so I start with the top left drawer of the card catalog.

I will page everything until I find her. The sky darkens
as the librarian brings cart after cart of headstones
and hardtack, wildflower and birds' nests, beer cans

and scuffed home plates. They bring
my browning boutonnière, bunting, firecrackers,
floats stuck with stale candy. They bring

ledgers and epaulets, apiaries and haystacks,
my sister's basketball stats from sophomore year.
the gingham ghost of a girl in halter dress, silver

dangling from her ears, lace on her hem. I finger
lures in a tin tackle box. A fishing line
catches my cuff and tautens, leading me

into the hush of algae-slicked stacks where fish
tap silver tails on the wet floor gasping
their last. The line loops my wrists and snakes

down my back, circling my waist, cuts the corners
of my mouth, forcing my head back. I fall
to my knees as the automatic lights click off

down the rows as if the archive is counting
to a hundred before it throws me back.

what the archive hides in its benthic dark

The Archivist unwinds the line in the dark—their motion unde-tected by the lights' sensors—and lifts me from the floor. They guide me down narrow stairs, the only illumination comes from the moon of their palms. Tripping over the hooves of a musk ox, I realize we are in the taxidermy collection. The mannequin spearing a fish is gone, replaced by a girl, not quite fifteen, in cut-offs and her grandfather's shirt, so big she has to tie it at the waist. She clutches a trout in her two fists, staring into its plastic eye. The Archivist lifts the glass surface of the water, and we dive into the acrylic pond beneath.

Jellyfish, attracted to the glow of the Archivist's palms, swarm; their shrouds cosset our skin. They trail us as we swim past Pose-idon dozing with nameless sea gods of forgotten civilizations, ancient creatures mostly mouth, Aristotle's unadorned shark, and the diving bell where Alexander watched a creature so large it took three days to swim by. We pass the lab bench my sister was forced to share with me when she repeated biology, squid pinned opened on the tray. Behind a row of jarred eels doubled into pouting parabolas, the Archivist retrieves an unaccessioned box and leads be back up, pulling the line like a leash. I want to ask them about the box, but my mouth is crammed with hooks.

That night I dream I am being rocked through the ocean in a squid's embrace, listening to the laconic clicks of whales. When I stroke her mantel, her skin splits under my hands' scalpels and her giant nerve slides out in a web of veins. Blood plunges me into darkness as I am strangled by her paroxysms. I wake up, gasping. The box regards me from the dresser. Inside I find por-celain bells and glass ornaments, so delicate they crack in the air, powder under my touch. All I hold is wire, twisted to suspend clappers or hook around a branch. As the powder drifts away, the wire remains, stubborn as siblings.

the archive tells you you are in the wrong war

with Daisy to display his purety, the red D
stares up at me from my sister's paper on
The Great Gadsby. I riffle through my notes.
I thought I'd paged military records--western
Pennsylvania--minor conflicts. *Come on,*
she begs. *Please help me. I need at least a B
to graduate.*

         She kneels outside the bathroom door,
hands steepled in prayer as I apply band-aids
to my bleeding heels. *I'm sorry I told
grandpa about your outfit.* The taxidermy
collection's mannequins model Junior Miss
fashions, and our next-door neighbor tells me
I just haven't found *the right fit.* I am trussed
with measuring tape, and the card catalog spills

lace, those tiny bows at the center of everything.
I'll help you walk in those shoes, my sister bargains.
They will break in, I promise.

         Two cocktails
in at my grandfather's wake, she wraps me
in her arms. *I'm just so glad* she drools
into my suitcoat, *You seem happy finally
now that you're...you know...yourself.*

Once, the only god I had was my sister
and like every god she turned away. Now
the archive is a giant lung, wheezing
with the breath of unsaid things. I study men—
their acts of war, their books on civilization,

their achievements. They bind their records
in leather, paint the pages with gilt. They invented
the system I use to find them and yet
my page slips keep turning up girls'
diaries, mixtapes from car pools, our voices
shouting *love you like a sister always*, the flyer
from the concert we snuck into with fake
IDs, the note I never replied to *I am frightened
of what they will do to us if*

QB 468
.W48x
W5   Unknown
       possible utterances--unpublished non-commercial
       recording--open reel magnetic tape--1948-1980--1/4"
       Magnetic tape (polyester-based tape with ferromagnetic
       particles embedded in binder layer) wound onto 7" diameter
       plastic reel with slotted hub--7 ½ ips

trapping equipment and supplies
see also: capture-based aquaculture
see also: escapement (fisheries)

precipitation (meteorology) --united states--history--19th and 20th century

see also: melt water
see also: thawing

see also: wind-snow interaction
see also: depth hoar

skeleton--north america--identification
osteology

fire extinction--equipment and supplies--history
narrower term: command and control at fires
narrower term: fire streams
narrower term: hose-couplings

activities of daily living--united states
see also: activities of daily living--handbooks

rape--united states--history
sex crimes--united states--history
rape as weapon of war--history
united states--history--20th century
historical reenactments

QB 468
.W48x
W5

We are only shuttling information. The information comes to us as if we are looking to the sky and seeing the flash of white on the underside of a wing.

Comes as seven hoof prints left by deer in the mud where the camp once stood.

We are only the mud, unmarked next to the historical site, where the second-year history student dresses as a local woman to show how they did laundry back then.

Back then a funny time when people boiled their clothes.

Back then before the Americans built the road all the way up the mountain.

We are only imprints speckled along a typewriter platen.

There the general typed: *I can't keep my men from the refugee women.*

He typed: *And with the impossibilities of getting supplies, we need to choose*

We are only three men's memory as they lean against a Jeep choosing in a surprising spring snow.

Only a general's memory of women's voices—the voices themselves vanished.

We are only the vanishing of snow.

Only the fistful of snow the woman crams in her mouth to
extinguish her memory.

The fistful of snow the woman crams in her mouth to
distinguish this day from the others.

The snow the woman crams in her mouth to stop her own
screaming.

We are only the drift of her body in the current.

Only the memory of eels, cradling her body as it sinks and the
prayer of eels curled among the bones.

Only the comfort of eels, sliding through her ribs to remember.

We are only water and we could not rise up without rain, rise
up and save her.

Instead we offer memory and our memory is only as good as our
archive where her name is not written, her death unremarked,
her number uncounted.

We are only the blanks of women and we carry these blanks
inside us as the sky carries the white beneath a wing.

and in the end the archive keeps its own council

I came to the archive looking for blame
to cut like a furrow and instead I am
received, unbounded, and mended,

lain on the Archivist's table, where they measure
my ear, the circumference of its shadow.
Like paper, skin absorbs all—each tap

of the service bell, every knuckle crushed
into a fist, all the milkweed rolled between palms,
silk unspooling. The Archivist sweeps

a cloth through the gully of my collarbone, thumbs
my spine looking for give, where it needs
repair. They fold muslin under my neck, bolster

tender joints, and tip open my jaw, lift
my tongue to read the utterances lodged
in my throat. For my entry, they weave

my present into description using a logic I can
only submit to as we float in the archive's tank
of dreams, bodies stitched together with a dash.

See Also

Cvetkovich, Ann. *An Archive of Feelings: Trauma, Sexuality,*
 and Lesbian Public Cultures.
 Durham,NC: Duke University Press, 2003.

Muñoz, José Esteban. "Ephemera as Evidence: Introductory
 Notes to Queer Acts." *Women &Performance: A*
 Journal of Feminist Theory, vol. 8, no. 2, pp. 5-16.
 http://dx.doi.org/10.1080/0740770960857. Accessed
 8 Nov. 2009.

Singh, Julietta. *No Archive Will Restore You.* 3Ecologies Books/
 Immediations, an Imprint of Punctum Books, 2018.

Acknowledgments

I would like to thank the editors the following journals in which poems from this collection have appeared: *Narrative* ("the archive is all in present tense") and *The Baffler* ("QB 468. W 48x W5," "TJ 1015 .H66" and their accompanying card catalogue entries).

"Found in Collection" was inspired by "The Voyage of the Sable Venus" by Robin Coste Lewis.

I'd like to acknowledge the influence of poet and my first mentor Michael S. Harper (1938-2016), who introduced me to the poetic potentials of archives by sending me to the John Hay Library at Brown University where rumors swirled about a book bound in human skin. My mentor and friend Catherine Bowman's influence is also all over this book, particularly because she always encourages me to push form using my own ear and instinct.

Before that, my parents—Bob Hoover and Susan Yohe—took me and my sisters to the Carnegie Museums of Art and Natural History and the Carnegie Library of Pittsburgh. I credit them for my love of dioramas and my confusion over disciplinary separation. I'd also like to thank both my sisters: Dorothy Hoover, for her patience and creative vision when an earlier version of *the archive is all in present tense* was launched as a performance and for creating the image for the cover of the book, and Margaret Hoover, for attending my readings even when they started absurdly late in dive bars and required her to pay a babysitter.

Finally, to Jackson Alexander Lennox for his unflagging encouragement and miraculous love.

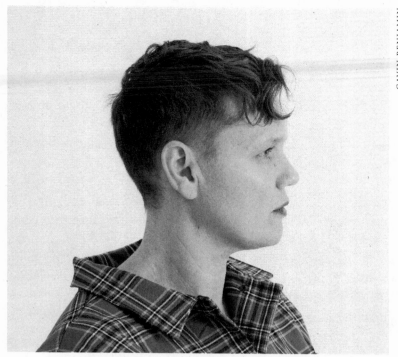

GAVIN BENJAMIN

Poet and essayist **ELIZABETH HOOVER** was born and raised in Pittsburgh. Her poetry has appeared in *Prairie Schooner*, *The Crab Orchard Review*, and *Tupelo Quarterly*, among others, and her nonfiction has been published in the *North American Review*, *Kenyon Review*, and *StoryQuarterly*. She teaches at Webster University in St. Louis.

BARROW STREET POETRY

Heterotopia
Lesley Wheeler 2010

This Noisy Egg
Nicole Walker 2010

Black Leapt In
Chris Forhan 2009

Boy with Flowers
Ely Shipley 2008

Gold Star Road
Richard Hoffman 2007

Hidden Sequel
Stan Sanvel Rubin 2006

Annus Mirabilis
Sally Ball 2005

A Hat on the Bed
Christine Scanlon 2004

Hiatus
Evelyn Reilly 2004

3.14159+
Lois Hirshkowitz 2004

Selah
Joshua Corey 2003